Illustrated By

Kaya Beale

Written By

Stacey Dyer

Published in association with
Bear With Us Productions

ISBN: 978-1-5272-9412-7

Cover by Richie Evans
Design by Luisa Moschetti
Illustrated by Kaya Beale

www.justbearwithus.com

For Charlie, and all who threw his ball

And for Adam, Matilda and Jude, who will still probably prefer to read The Gruffalo, but thanks for always loving me, you're everything to me.

Look out for the ladybird hidden on each page! 

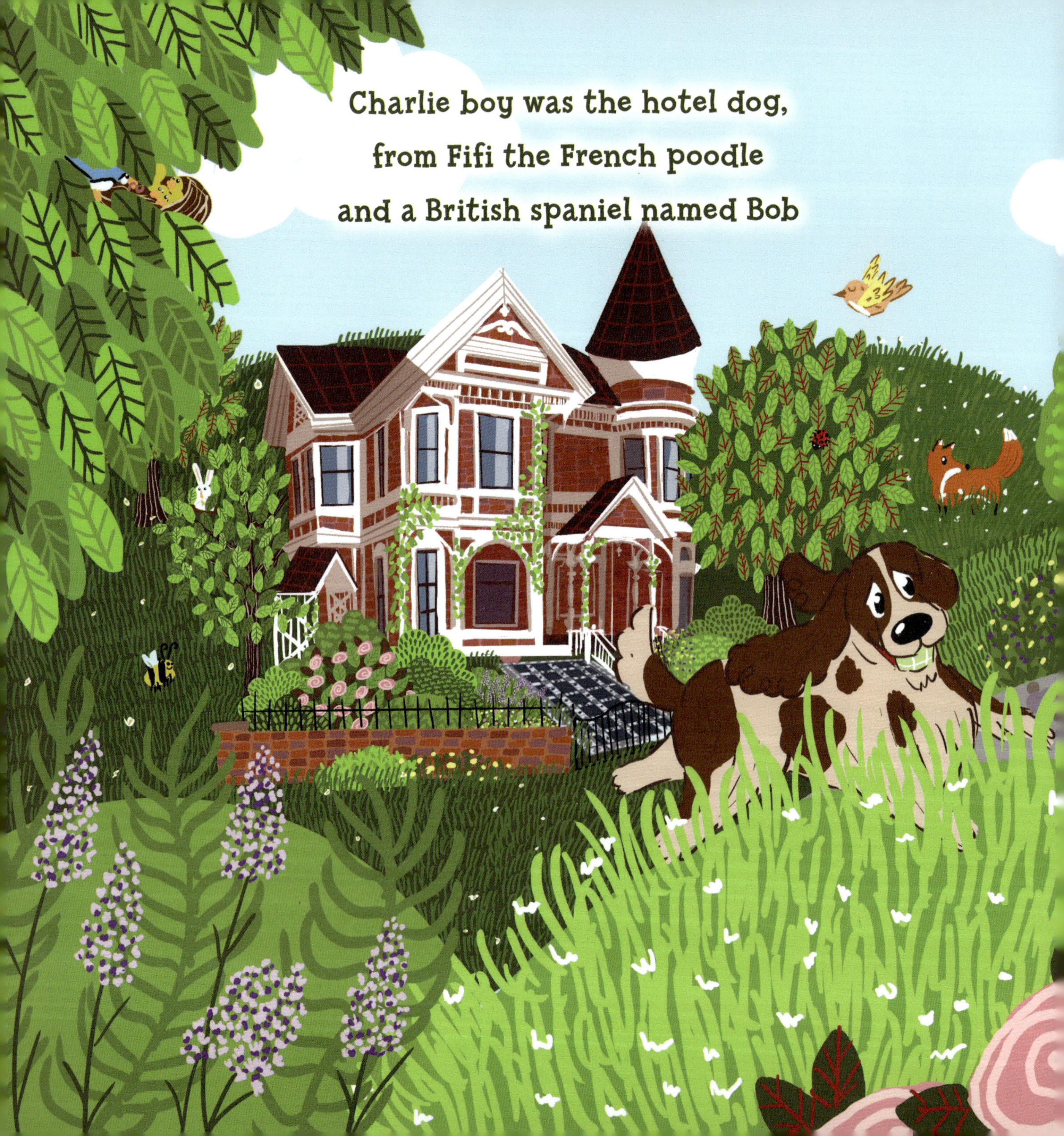

Charlie boy was the hotel dog,
from Fifi the French poodle
and a British spaniel named Bob

Reception

Now Charlie loved to mingle with the hotel guests,
meeting new friends and hearing their tales
were his all time favourite and simply the best

What they liked for their tea,
what they wore on their feet,

how things looked in their land
and what they did for a treat

Tommie was Dutch and so much fun.

He played the guitar and wore his hair in a bun.

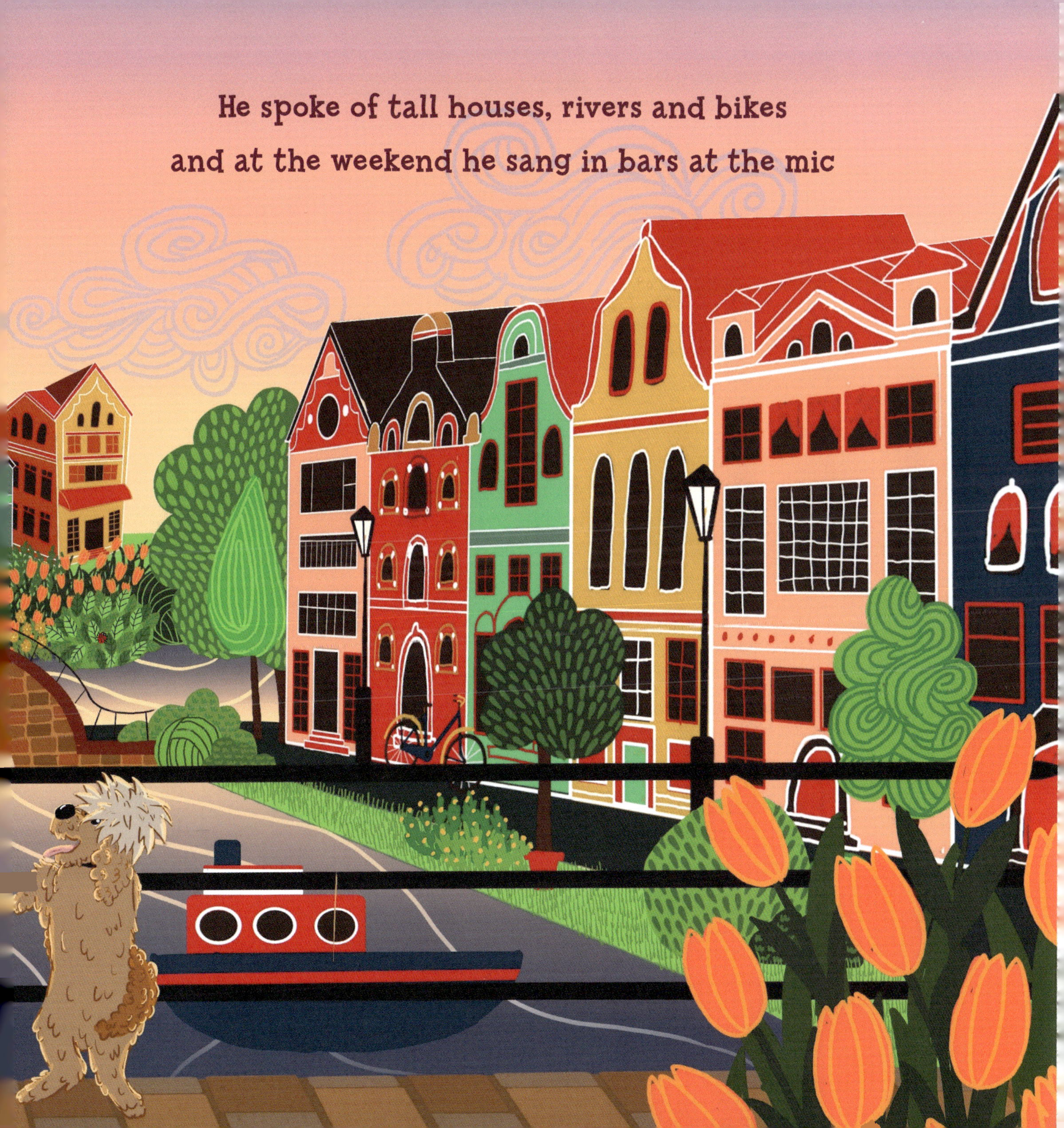

He spoke of tall houses, rivers and bikes
and at the weekend he sang in bars at the mic

Emily from Canada,
right up in the mountains,
was used to the snow
and icy fountains.

She watched ice hockey, ate curds and ski'd
and could spot a bear hiding from behind the trees

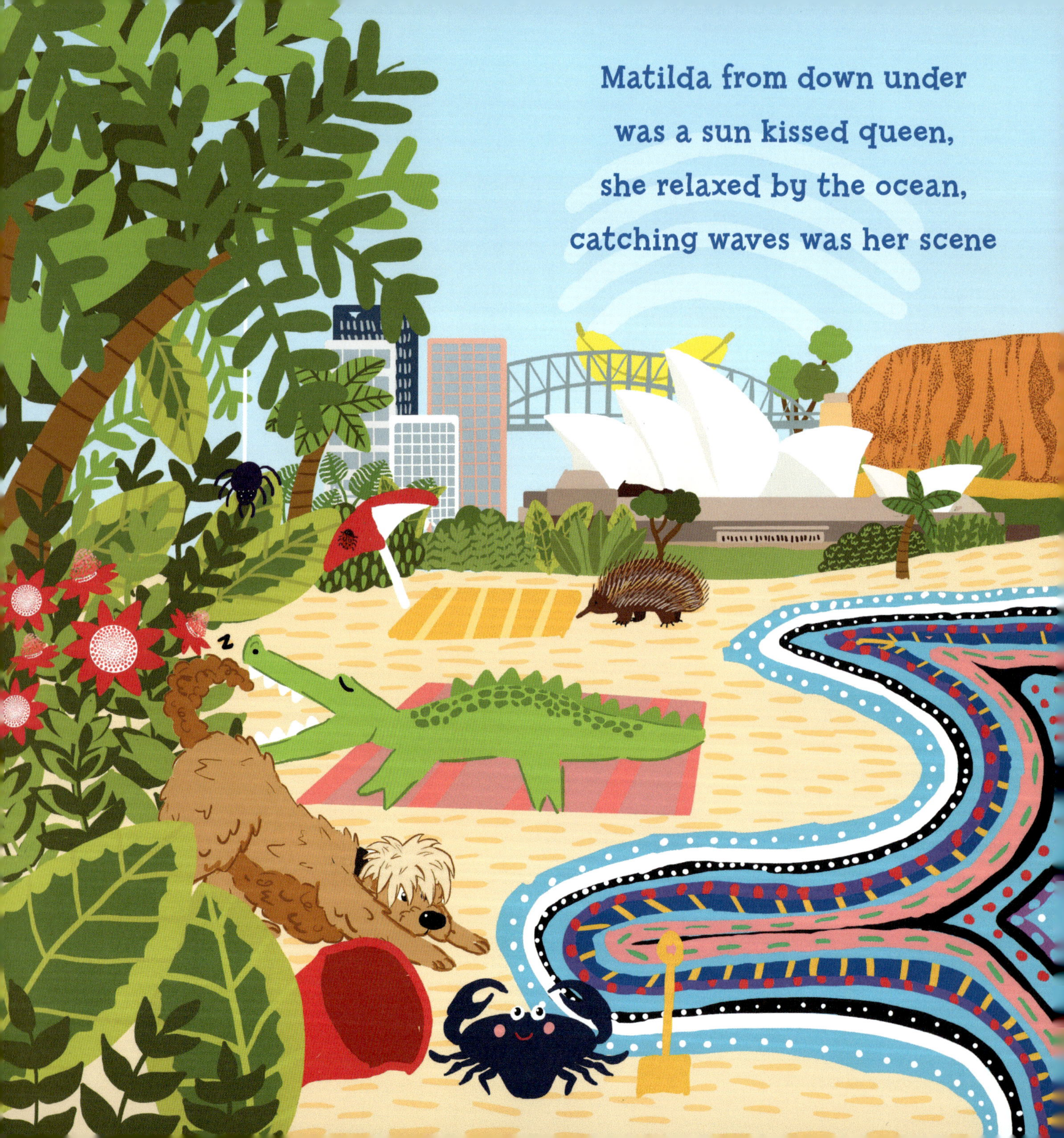

Matilda from down under
was a sun kissed queen,
she relaxed by the ocean,
catching waves was her scene

Never afraid of the sharks,
spiders or crocs
she lived in the sunshine
in flip flops (no socks)

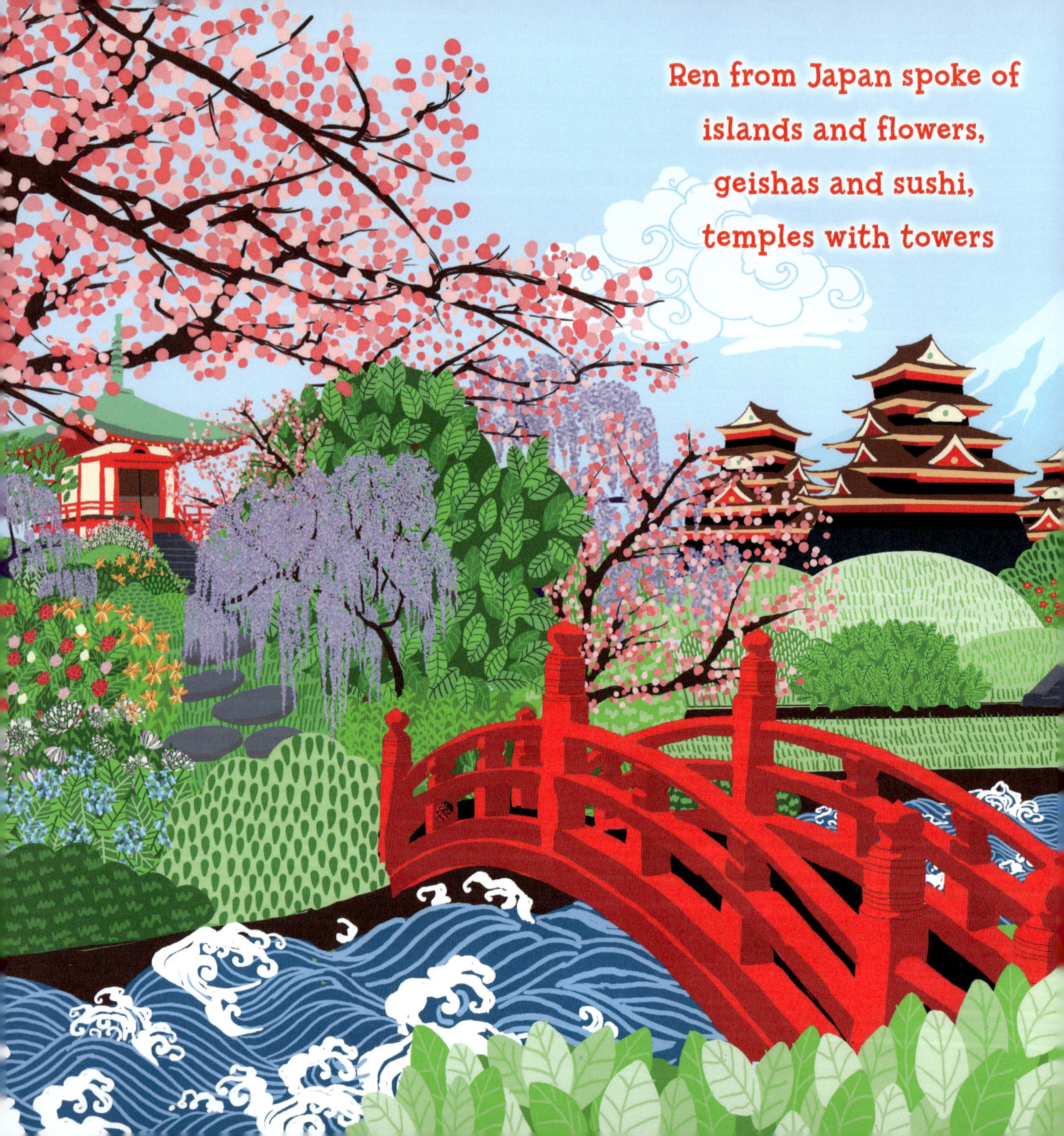

Ren from Japan spoke of
islands and flowers,
geishas and sushi,
temples with towers

Speeding trains
and blossom trees,
it sounded a place Charlie
definitely should see

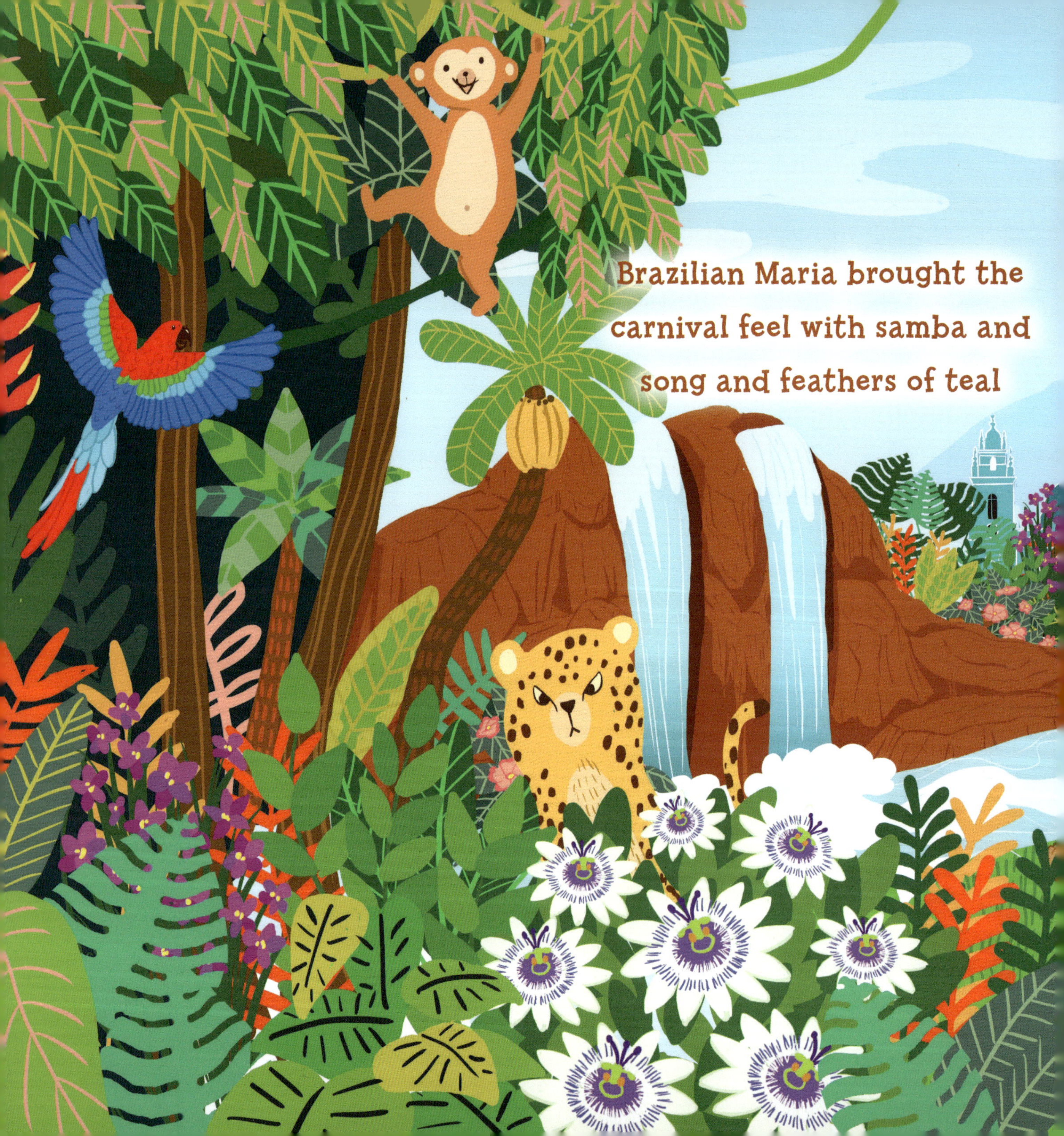

Brazilian Maria brought the carnival feel with samba and song and feathers of teal

Rainforests with tree frogs, sloths and plants
and howler monkeys with their noisy loud chants

Jude from Great Britain
was the joker in town,
never a dull moment,
never a frown

Roast dinners, the queen, rolling hills full of green.
Four seasons a day, bluebells in may,
wellies and sun hats were often the way

Charlie moved from room to room
sitting and listening

to the merry tune, of exotic accents
and traveller tales from far away lands all under one moon

He knew deep down although different and unique,
we're all the same, whichever language we speak

Be kind and open, generous and warm be friendly
and welcoming not quick to conform

All were welcome in Charlie's place, lively and fun, it was a comfortable space, for a week or a month, for an hour passing by, if there's a story to be told then Charlie's near by

Printed in Great Britain
by Amazon

69290558R00017